Whittling the Old Sea Captain and Crew

by

Mike Shipley

Fox Chapel Publishing Co Inc.

Box 7948
Lancaster, PA 17604

© 1996 by Fox Chapel Publishing Company, Inc.

Publisher: Alan Giagnocavo
Project Editor: Ayleen Stellhorn
Desktop Specialist: Bob Altland, Altland Design
Cover Photography: Bob Polett, VMI Communications

ISBN # 1–56523–075–2

Printed in Hong Kong

To order your copy of this book
please send check or money order
for $12.95 plus $2.50 to:
Fox Chapel Book Orders
Box 7948
Lancaster, PA 17604–7948

Try your favorite book supplier first!

Table of Contents

Foreword

The characters in this book are designed to be fairly simple and, above all, fun to carve. Anytime I choose a piece to carve, the number one thing in my mind is, "Will I enjoy carving it?" If I have to struggle with a piece, the enjoyment pretty well disappears.

These characters are not what you might call "action figures," they are just enjoyable to carve. They can be altered to be several different kinds of characters if you like. If you don't like the size, find a copy machine. Sometimes enlarging or reducing a pattern can completely change your outlook on a carving.

I would suggest carving all the characters, the buoys, the lobster traps and the other accessories. Find a piece of small mesh netting and use the carvings to create your own scene. If you have limited shelf space, just reduce the patterns and make a smaller scene.—*Mike Shipley*

Photo Gallery

The Old Sea Captain & His Crew

The Old Sea Captain

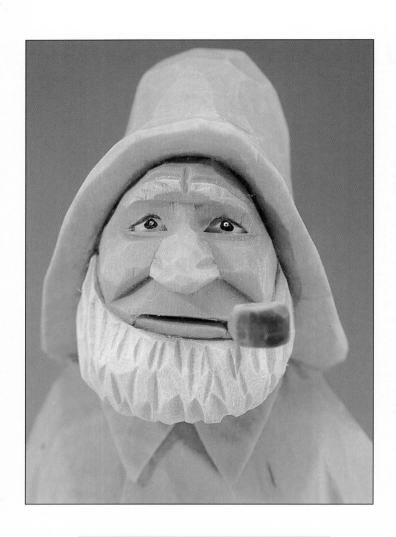

The Old Sea Captain is a very serious guy. He's seen a lot of long days at sea. But whether the seas be calm or stormy, or the fishing be good or bad, his confidence never wavers. A captain is only as good as his crew, and from the looks of his first and second mate, this captain has his hands full.

The captain's beard is very full–probably from being out at sea so long. As you carve the facial features, be sure to leave plenty of extra wood along the chin and jaw line to accommodate the captain's bushy beard. I use a 2 mm v-tool to detail the beard. Make lots of different length cuts. Some lines should be wavy to give the illusion of real whiskers. These same techniques can be used on the mustaches, eyebrows and hair of the other characters.

The First Mate

The first mate has one purpose in life, and that's to squeeze all the work he can out of the second mate. When he says jump, the second mate asks how high. He's tough, but underneath it all he's just an old softy.

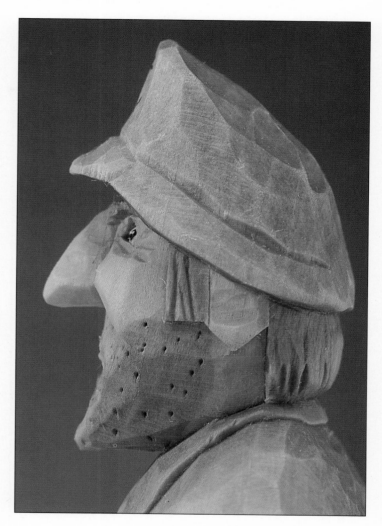

For many carvers, hands are one of the toughest areas to carve successfully. Putting a character's hands in his pockets is a simple way to reduce the difficulty of a piece. Simply carve a bulge under the material of the coat or pants to indicate the presence of a hand in the pocket. More advanced carvers may want to alter the patterns in this book so that the hands are visible or even holding a buoy or some other object.

The Second Mate

The second mate enjoys life and doesn't have a care in the world, except when the first mate is watching. The two of them have been through everything from 100-foot waves to being stranded on a desert island, but like any good crew they stick together.

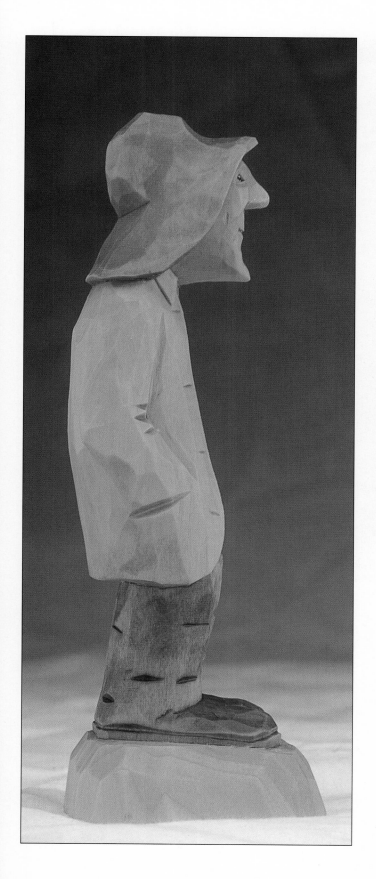

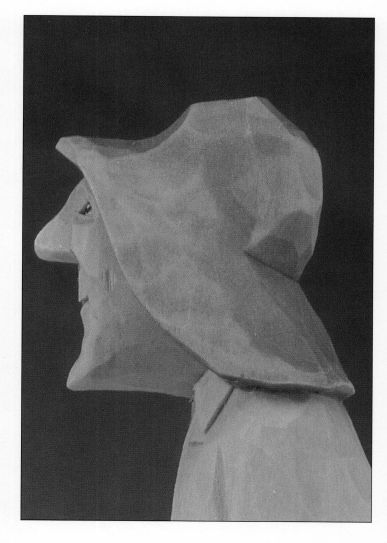

Buttons can be made any number of ways. One of the quickest ways to make a perfectly shaped button is to use an eye punch. I often use a $\frac{1}{8}$" eye punch, but you can use larger or smaller sized punches for differently sized buttons. To make the button, push the tool gently but firmly into the wood. Apply just enough pressure to make a visible circle. Add some paint, and you have a nicely rounded button.

The Accessories

Lobster traps, crates, buoys and oars are all perfect accessories for your Old Sea Captain and his crew. These simple items can be carved easily out of scrap pieces of wood. Use other props, such as netting or a boat, to make the scene even more realistic.

Carving the Old Sea Captain

Before You Begin

I use a variety of tools, but for these projects you won't need many tools. Medium price-range tools work very well. The tools listed below will be all the tools you'll need to finish the projects in this book.

Bench knife

10mm v-tool

2mm v-tool

3mm u-gouge

Awl

Fine-tipped bench knife

⅛ Eye punch

I will be using basswood for the old captain and his crew. Although other woods will work just as well, basswood is always my first choice for carvings of this size.

It's important to not let a blade get too dull between each sharpening. A blade should be sharpened and shaped on a stone. When it dulls, buff it on a bench grinder with a cotton or cloth buffing wheel coated with jeweler's rouge buffing compound. A blade can be buffed several times before using a stone. The buffing provides a good, quick cutting edge and saves excess wear on the blade.

Safety is an important part of carving. Whether you're a beginner or an old pro, always take a minute before you begin to consider your own safety. Always keep your knife sharp. Always keep control of your tool. And always keep your fingers out of the way!

1. First trace the side view on a block of basswood. Using a bandsaw or a coping saw, cut as close to the lines as possible. Always saw the side view first. Leave enough wood on the back of the head and base to make the blank lie flat on the bandsaw table. This will make the blank more stable when sawing the front view.

The Old Sea Captain • 1

2. Trace the front view on the blank. Remember to saw as close to the lines as possible. Now let's get busy.

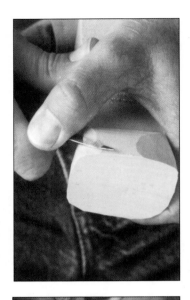

3. Start by rounding the corners of the base with a bench knife. Continue rounding the base until it is well proportioned all the way around.

4. Now start rounding the coat. Because of the grain, carve down toward the base. Finish rounding the coat on all sides. Use your thumb pressure to regulate the amount of wood that you remove. Constant thumb pressure also helps you to control the blade, preventing accidents.

5. Next round the coat on the upper body and shoulders. You'll notice that I change the position of the carving throughout this demonstration. Hold the carving in a position that is comfortable for you and works well with the grain.

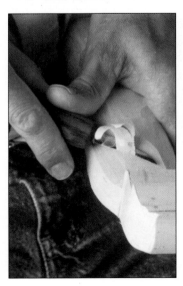

6. Round the coat up under the chin and finish the upper body. With these rounding steps, we are just basically removing the rough, sawed surface.

7. After the coat is rounded, move up to the head and round the hat. Don't cut to the shape of the hat yet—just remove the sawed surface of the wood.

8. Move down to the boots and knock off the edges of the blank below the bottom of the coat.

9. Finish rounding the boots, but don't try to finish the boots completely yet. All we want to do now is get the general shape of the boots.

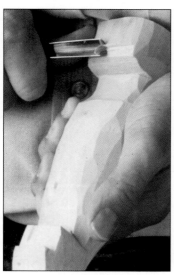

10. With a 10mm v-tool, cut a line all the way around where the boot soles join the base. Make sure the base height is the same all the way around.

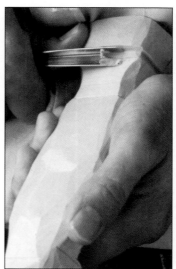

11. Remove more wood around the line to shape the boots a little more. The boot toes will be separated, so leave some extra wood in front.

12. Now with the captain roughed out, we can start with some details. Pencil on the arms on both sides. Take care to get the arms proportional with each other.

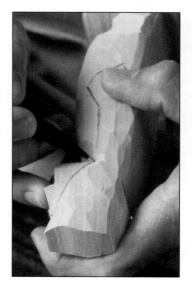

13. The brim should drop slightly around the sides of the face. Pencil on a line to indicate where the hat brim meets the face.

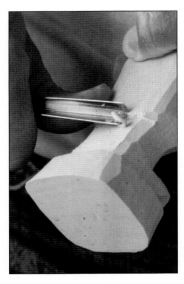

14. Cut a line around the bottom of the coat with the large v-tool. Make sure the coat is even on all sides.

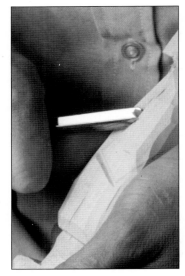

15. With the large v-tool, cut the pencil lines to outline the arms. Start cutting these lines deeper to bring out the arms. Because the coat is loose-fitting, the arms will not be too prominent.

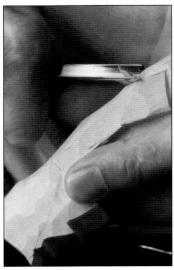

16. Roughly shape the arms, front and back.

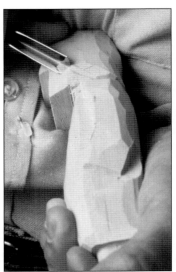

17. Cut the line around the hat brim. Then remove some wood under the hat brim on the sides of the head. Notice the face will be more narrow at the top.

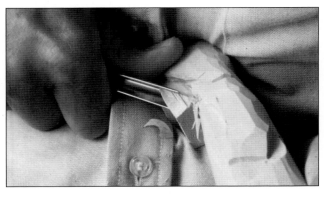

18. Continue roughing in the face on both sides. As you rough in the face, keep checking the proportions of the face on both sides.

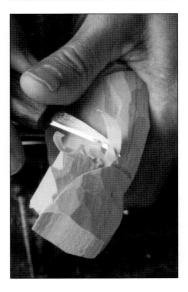

19. Now clean up a little with a bench knife. Don't try to finish the face now. Just rough it in at this point.

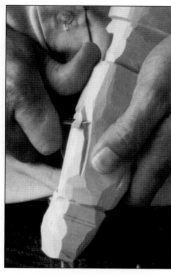

20. Clean up the arms with a knife.

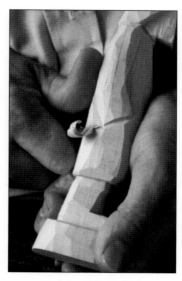

21. Remove some wood on the coat to bring out the arms.

22. Clean up both arms and compare them for the same proportions. Are both arms the same width and length?

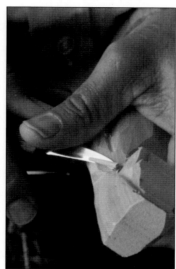

23. Remove wood from the shoulders under the hat brim.

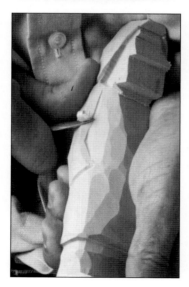

24. Shape the arms up to the shoulders and under the hat.

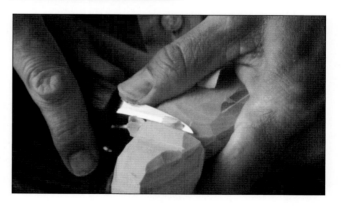

25. Clean up under the hat on all sides.

The Old Sea Captain • 5

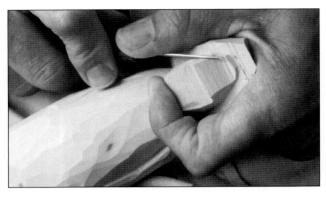

26. With a bench knife, shape the face until the dimensions look natural. After a few more cuts here the face will be a nice size.

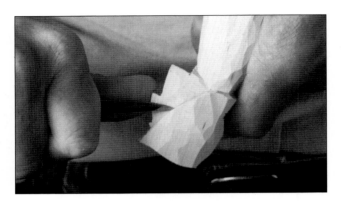

27. With the knife tip cut around the face and hat.

28. Clean up under the hat brim. Use thumb pressure on the back of the blade to control the knife. I don't want to damage the hat brim... or my fingers.

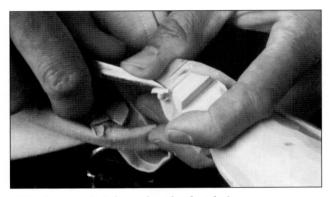

29. As you finish under the hat brim remove some extra wood in a couple places to make the brim look wavy or droopy.

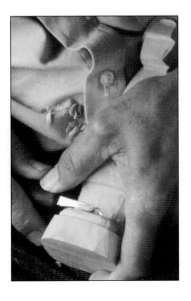

30. Next, work all around the boots until they start shaping up. On the front of the boots remove a small amount of wood next to the foot to give the boots some shape. We want to avoid making the boots come straight down to the foot. Clean up the top of the feet.

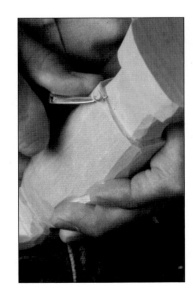

31. Clean up around the bottom of the coat.

32. Now back to the head again. I move all over a carving like this during the roughing-in process so all areas of the piece will be at the same stage.

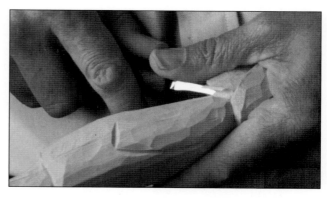

33. Start cleaning up under the jaw and beard area. Cut away the sawed surfaces so the area where the beard meets the jaw is smooth and rounded.

34. Be careful to leave enough wood for eyebrows. Round the forehead under the hat brim.

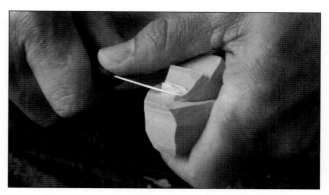

35. Clean up the eyebrow enough to leave a good ridge of wood.

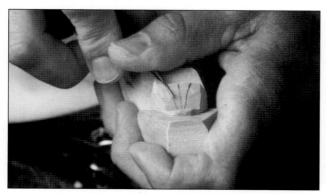

36. Pencil on a rough nose. Then, with a bench knife, cut straight in to outline the nose.

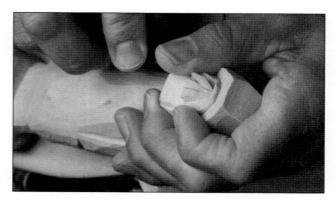

37. Remove wood on each side of the nose and clean up each side. Using thumb pressure to control the blade is very important when working on the face. If you make cuts that are too deep, you may not be able to work them out when you finish the face.

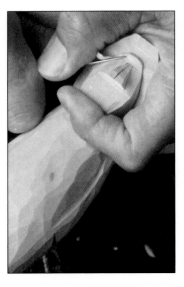

38. Round the edges of the face on each side.

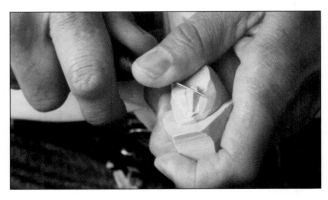

39. Start shaping the nose by cutting the bottom corner on each side.

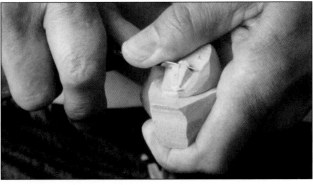

40. Shape the bottom of the nose next. Remember, a nose is longer in the middle and slightly shorter on each side.

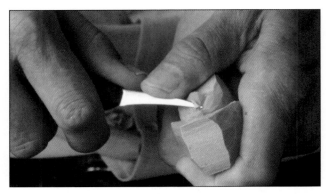

41. Now round the nose slightly and clean it up a little.

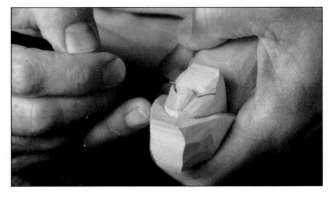

42. Before marking on the cheek lines, make sure the outside corners of the nose are cut in shorter than the middle of the nose. Then pencil on the cheek line from the outer edge of the face to the outside corners of the nostrils.

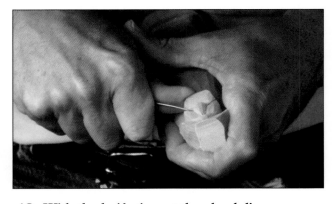

43. With the knife tip, cut the cheek lines.

44. Cut straight in at the nostril and cheek.

45. Cut the other side to match.

46. Now remove some wood up to the cheek.

47. Take the cut in pretty deep to raise the cheek and round the mouth and lip areas.

48. Clean up the mouth area. The mouth should appear raised and slope deeply over to the cheeks.

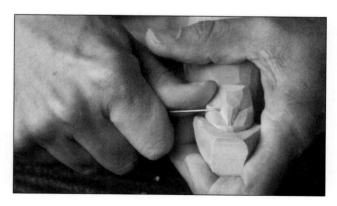

49. Round and shape the cheeks.

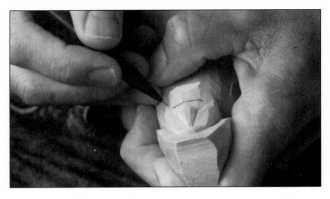

50. Pencil on the mouth. The captain won't have much of a smile.

51. With a knife, cut the line fairly deep. Remove a thin sliver of wood at the bottom of the cut to separate the upper and lower lips.

52. Cut in at each corner of the mouth.

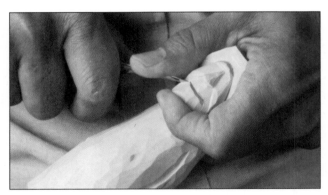

53. Notice the cut at each corner of the mouth. With the knife tip, cut in to each cut. This will tuck the lip into each corner of the mouth.

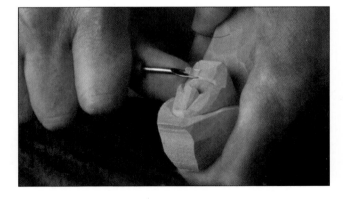

54. With a 3mm u-gouge, make a cut across just under the lower lip to raise the lip.

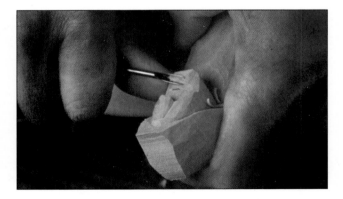

55. Deepen the area under the lip with the u-gouge.

56. Now use a knife to clean up around the beard area.

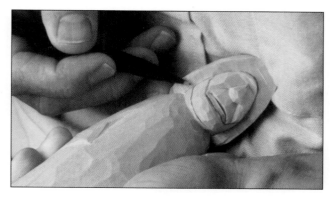

57. After shaping the beard area, pencil on the actual beard lines. The beard will flow up on the cheeks and just under the bottom lip.

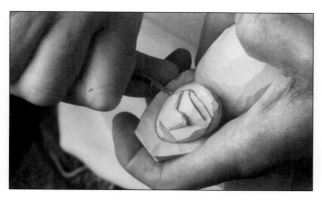

58. With the knife tip, cut in the beard lines.

59. Using the cut line as a stop, remove wood on the neck under the beard. The neck area will be covered with the material of the coat.

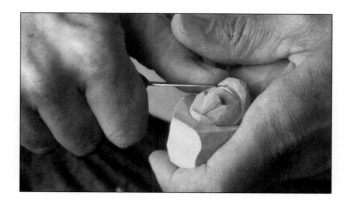

60. Remove wood along the cheeks to raise the beard away from the face. Continue removing wood around the beard to clean it up.

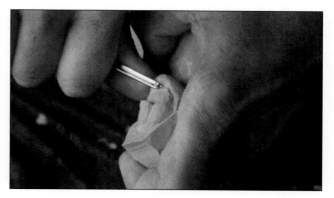

61. With a 2mm v-tool, cut across under the bottom lip to raise the lip a little more.

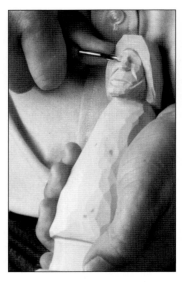

62. Now we're getting somewhere. With the 3mm u-gouge, scoop out the eye sockets. Just scoop out shallow egg-shaped sockets.

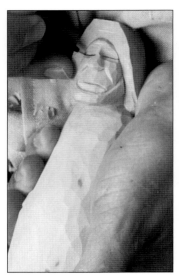

63. Pencil a straight line on each socket. This will be the lower eyelid. Make sure the lids are even on both sides. It is very easy to get the eyes mismatched or cross-eyed. The eyes usually make or break a carving, so take the time to get the pencil marks right before you make any cuts.

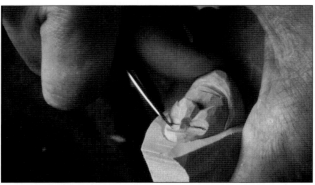

64. With the knife tip, cut the line. Then cut a half moon above. You might want to pencil in the half moon shape before cutting.

65. On the other side, cut the line for the lower eyelid.

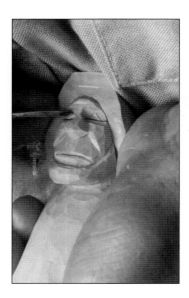

66. Then cut a half moon above the line, just like the other side. Again, make sure both shapes match.

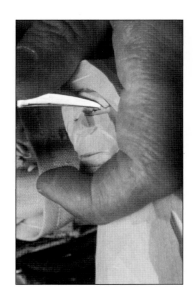

67. Now gently trim away the outside corner of the eyeball.

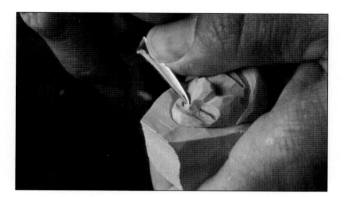

68. Trim away the inside corner of the eyeball.

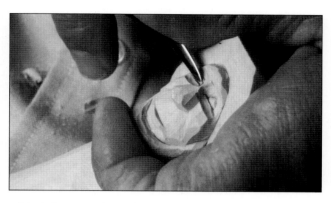

69. Move to the other eye. Trim the inside corner of the eyeball. Then trim the outside corner of the eyeball.

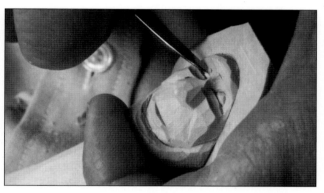

70. Now trim and clean up the edges around the eyeball to round the eyeballs.

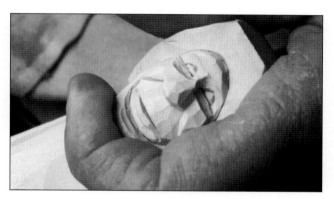

71. Check the proportion of the eyes. You can still do a little trimming if the eyes do not quite match.

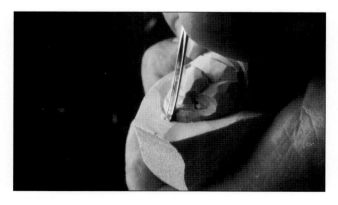

72. With the 2mm v-tool, make a cut right between the eyes to separate the eyebrows.

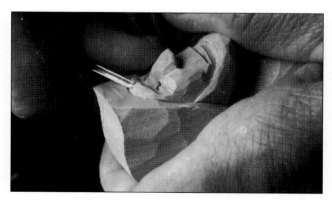

73. Make a cut across the top of the eyebrows.

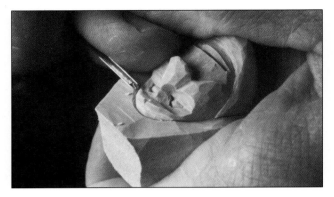

74. Make the cut deep enough to raise the eyebrows off the face.

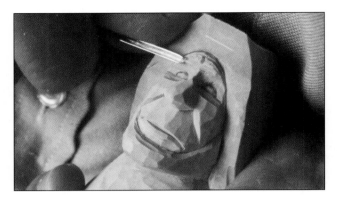

75. Make small cuts in the eyebrow to create lines for the eyebrow hair.

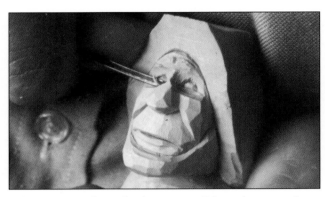

76. To complete the lower eyelid, make a cut just under the lower eyelid. There's no need to make an upper eyelid. Just a simple line cut across will form the lower eyelid.

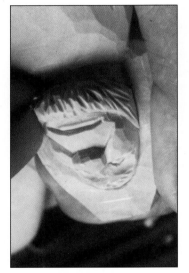

77. Now cut small lines to make beard hair. Make the cuts different lengths. Some lines should be made wavy to give the illusion of real hair or whiskers.

78. Pencil on the coat line to one side or the other. Draw a simple collar and pencil on the line separating the boots.

79. Cut straight into the lines of the collar and the coat. Remove wood next to the lines to raise the collar above the coat.

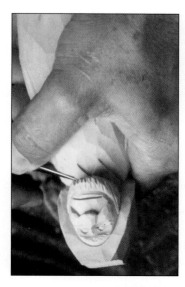

80. Notice the collar is just a simple V shape, the rest of the collar will disappear up under the hat brim.

81. Remove some wood along the coat opening to slightly raise it above the coat.

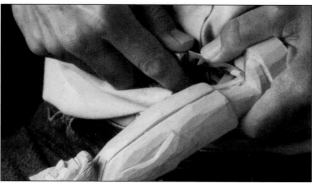

82. First separate the boots with a v-tool, then use a knife to clean up. Continue rounding the boots until they are well-shaped and proportional on each side.

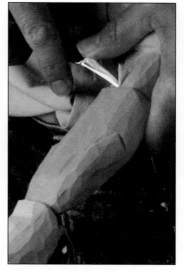

83. Cut a shallow line in the back of the piece to separate the boots.

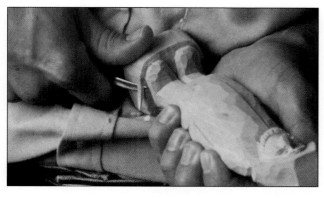

84. Now the boots are pretty well shaped. Remember, they don't have to be perfect; they are just large, loose-fitting rubber boots. Round the top edge of the base with a knife.

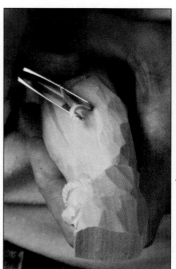

85. Use a large v-tool to do some final clean up around the arms. Do any additional clean up on the arms to make sure they match.

86. The arms should be slightly bent at the elbows. Make two or three cuts at each arm bend to make wrinkles in the sleeve.

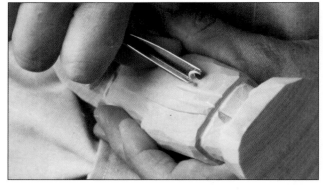

87. On the front at the bottom of the coat, make three or four bold cuts to make folds or wrinkles in the coat. Do the same on the back at the bottom of the coat.

88. With the bench knife, finish the hat. Leave the brim large. The hat should appear droopy.

89. With the hat pretty well finished, notice the wide brim.

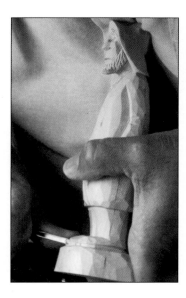

90. With a 2mm v-tool, cut around the boots to make boot soles.

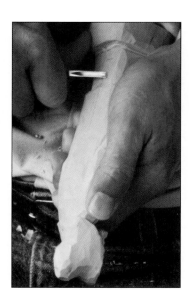

91. Make a few bold cuts in various places around the boots to make wrinkles.

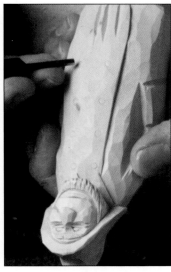

92. With a ⅛" eye punch, make the buttons on the coat. Punch two rows of four buttons. Apply just enough pressure to make a visible circle. You can cut the buttons with a knife tip, but the eye punch is much faster and easier.

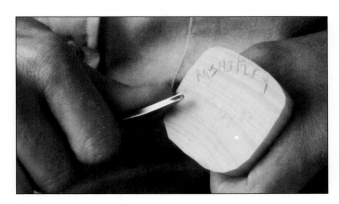

93. Now here's the best part. Sign the piece with a small v-tool.

94. With the small v-tool cut some crow's feet at the outside corners of the eyes. You might want to experiment and cut some wrinkles in other places, such as around the mouth.

95. With an awl, punch a hole at the corner of the mouth for the pipe.

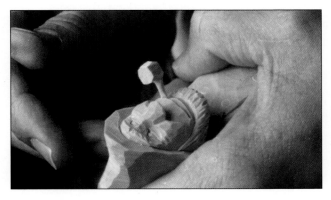

96. Carve the pipe with a knife until you are happy with the shape. Insert the pipe in the mouth, but don't glue it yet. You might have to adjust the hole or the pipe stem to get a good fit.

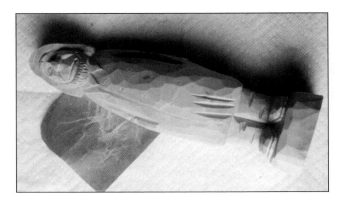

97. The carving is done. Check the captain over to see if he needs any minor adjustments. Finally, sand the piece lightly with 220-grit, very fine sandpaper to remove any surface dirt and give the piece a worn look.

Chapter Two
Painting

Painting
the
Old Sea Captain

Before You Begin

I used acrylic paints thinned with water to paint the Old Sea Captain. I thinned the paint down to almost a wash or water color.

Acrylics are very versatile. The great thing about acrylics is that you can thin them to any shade you want. Just use your imagination. I've tried expensive acrylic paints all the way down to the inexpensive craft acrylic paints and have been very happy with the results. The cheaper paints seem to have a larger variety of colors than the more expensive brands. I use small bottles and keep the colors mixed at all times.

Be aware that a little bit of paint goes a long way. When you brush on the paint, you will have to blend it around on the wood to get good, even coverage. If you just brush it on, the paint will look light, dark or streaky. Shake the paint container periodically. Some colors tend to separate after a few minutes. Also, note that acrylics dry very fast; I can paint an entire piece without waiting for the paint to dry.

I use pure red sable brushes. The red sable brushes seem to last better than most brushes. Just be sure to clean them well with water after every use. I'm still experimenting with the different brands; the tips of some brands fray after only a few uses.

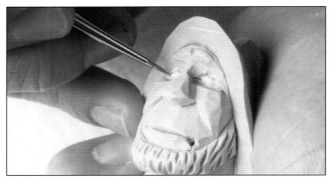

1. Use white for the eyeballs and a 4/0 spotter brush. There's not much room to paint, so take care not to paint the eyelids.

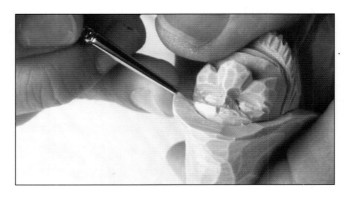

2. With the same spotter brush, paint the eyebrows white.

3. Paint the beard white with a #2 shader brush.

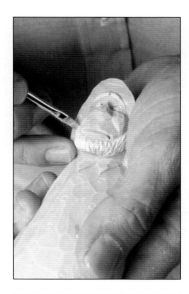

4. Work the paint into the whiskers.

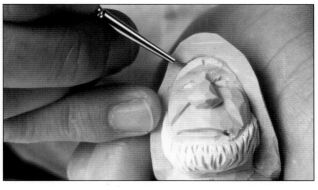

5. Now that we're finished with white on the face, it's time for some flesh color. There are several shades that can be used for skin color. I use flesh. Paint the color on the face with the #2 shader.

6. You might want to use a smaller brush when putting flesh color around the eyes and eyebrows. We're finished with the face for now.

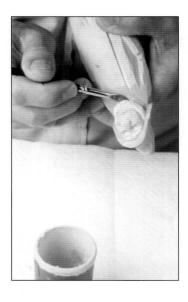

7. Paint the coat and the hat with medium yellow and a #6 shader brush. When painting this much surface, blend the paint on the wood to get good, even coverage.

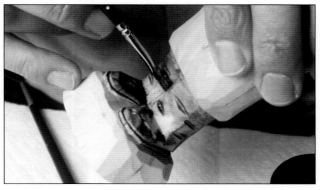

8. Paint the boots with black and the #6 shader.

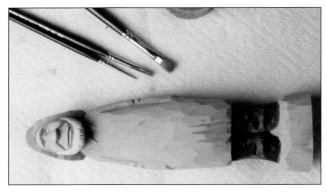

9. Looking good. So far, we've used a 4/0 spotter brush, a #2 shader brush and a #6 shader brush.

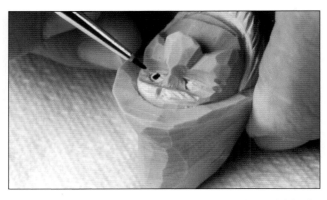

10. Paint the eyes with a spotter brush and black straight from the tube. Just dab a small dot on the eyeball and gently expand the dot until the eye looks natural and relaxed, not bug-eyed.

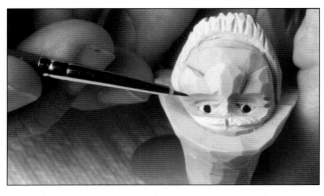

11. Paint both eyes and check for a match. Make any adjustments needed to make the eyes the same size.

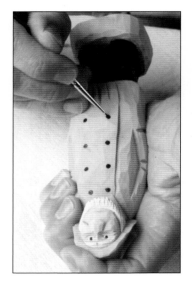

12. With the black, paint the buttons. You should be able to paint the imprint left by the eye punch quite easily. Paint eight buttons. But be careful. The buttons are very easy to smear.

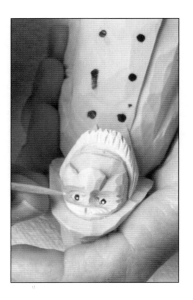

13. With white straight from the tube use a tooth pick to place a very small white dot on the black eye to highlight the eyeball. Oops, I told you the buttons were easy to smear. Pardon me while I go back and correct my mistake.

14. Now the captain is painted and ready to stain.

Staining the Old Sea Captain

Before You Begin

After you paint a piece with acrylics, notice how the colors have a bright and dry appearance. A stain will soften the colors. There are a lot of stains and finishes that you can use. I've tried most all of them; I even made my own with walnut hulls. That worked well until it started to ferment (and no, I didn't drink it).

Now I use boiled linseed oil and a small amount of raw umber oil paint. Another homemade mix, this one works quite well and doesn't ferment. I mix it in a quart-sized container. Remember to go easy with the raw umber oil paint; a little bit goes a long way. The stain requires a lot of shaking to get a good mix, but it's worth the effort.

Another added benefit of the stain is that the linseed oil will practically make the carving waterproof. When carvings sit on a shelf, they gather dust. With a linseed oil finish, I can just wash the carvings under the water faucet. After a piece is stained, the linseed oil will smell for a short time.

You can paint the stain on or, if the carving is small enough, just dip it in the stain and towel it dry with a paper towel. If you wish to brush the stain on, use any kind of brush with fairly soft bristles. Clean-up can be done with paint thinner or mineral spirits.

For this project, we'll be dipping the Old Sea Captain.

1. Usually the captain stands on deck and stays dry, but this time he's going to get dunked. Shake the stain well and just dunk him in.

2. Let the excess stain drip off for a minute.

3. Then turn the captain over and dunk the other half.

4. Again, let the excess drip off. Next dip the pipe.

5. Towel the captain dry with paper towels, and as simple as that, the staining is done.

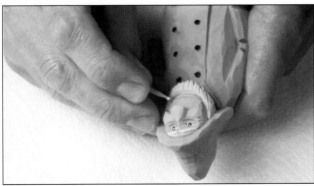

6. The captain is ready for a smoke, so it's time for the pipe. With the awl, repunch the hole in the corner of the mouth. Dab a small amount of wood glue on the pipe stem and insert the pipe. Hold the pipe in place for a minute until the glue sets.

7. Now it's time to sit back and enjoy our finished piece. You can use the patterns in Chapter Five to carve first and second mates for the captain. The information in Chapter Four gives you tips on creating lobster traps, buoys and other accessories for the captain and his crew.

Buoys, Lobster Traps & Oars

Before You Begin

Carving some accessories for the Old Sea Captain and his crew members will help to make any scene you create look more realistic. On the following page, I've included some brief instructions for carving lobster traps, two kinds of buoys, wooden crates and oars. You may want to take it a little further and carve some dock posts or flooring planks and even add a mesh net to the scene.

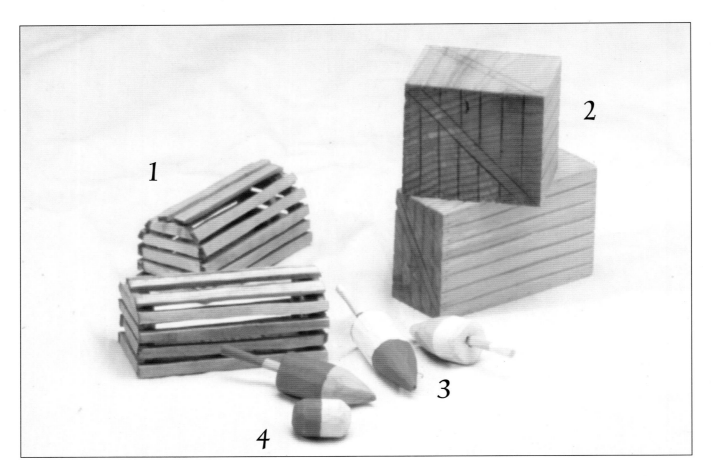

1. Lobster Traps

The lobster traps are the hardest and most time-consuming accessory to make. I made these traps from scrap pieces of wood. Lobster traps should look old and weathered, so every piece does not have to be perfect. These traps are 3 1/4 inches long, 1 1/2 inches wide and 1 1/2 inches high. The bottom is solid. The strips or slats can be slightly wider than 1/8 inch. I cut everything on a bandsaw. The frames for each end are u-shaped. Start by gluing the end frames to the bottom, then start gluing the slats from the bottom to the top. It takes a lot of time to make a lobster trap, but the trap will really add to the scene.

2. Wooden Crates

The wooden crates are just blocks of wood with some added details. I carved on boards and used a punch for the nail holes. You can make the crates any size you want.

3. Cone-shaped Buoys

The long cone-shaped buoys are 1 1/2 to 2 inches long. Just bring a cylinder-shaped piece of wood to a cone on one end. Leave the other end flat. Drill a small hole in the center of the flat end, sharpen a short piece of rounded wood, add some glue, and insert the wood into the hole. As you can see, you can paint the buoys any color you like. They are usually painted half one color and half another color.

4. Round Buoys

The small round buoys can be any size. Just round both ends, paint them half red and half white, and dip them in the stain.

Oars (Not pictured)

Oars add a nice touch and they are very easy to make. They will be 1/8 inch to 1/4 inch thick. I paint mine with very thin, dark green paint and dip them in stain. You could also skip the paint and just dip them in the stain.

The Old Sea Captain

The First Mate

3 x 2½ x 8

The Second Mate

Lobster Traps

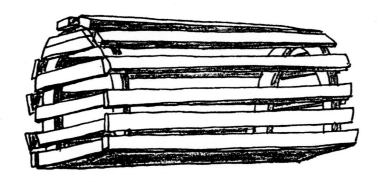

The lobster trap is hard to make, but it will be worth the trouble when it's finished. Make the trap from small strips of wood approximately $\frac{1}{8}$" thick. Remember a lobster trap should look old and probably in need of repair, so the strips don't have to be cut perfectly. Make the trap $3\frac{1}{4}$" long and $1\frac{1}{2}$" wide and $1\frac{1}{2}$" high. The bottom is solid, all pieces are $\frac{1}{8}$" thick; the strips or slats can be slightly wider than $\frac{1}{8}$". I cut everything on a bandsaw and clean up with a knife. The frame for each end is U-shaped. Start with the end frame and glue them to the bottom. Then start gluing the slats from the bottom to the top. Don't worry about gluing them all perfectly straight; it will look more realistic if some of the slats are crooked. When the glue is dry, dip the trap in stain and towel it dry.

CRATES

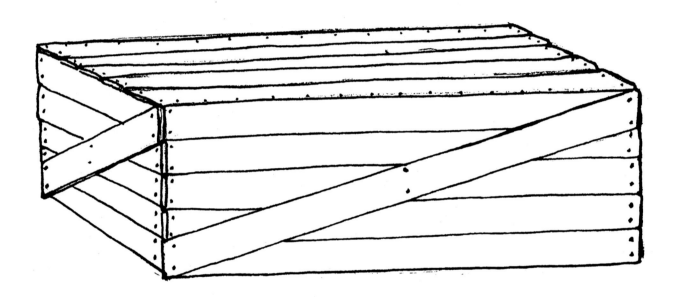

The crate is very easy to make. It is simply a block of wood with the boards indicated by carved lines. I use a small v-tool to make the lines and punch the nail holes with an awl. Make the crate any size you want. To finish the crate, dip it in stain and towel dry.

Buoys & Oars

To make the oars start with a thin piece of wood, 7" long, $\frac{1}{4}$" thick and $\frac{3}{4}$" wide. Don't worry about carving them perfectly: oars should look worn and weathered. Sand them with fine sandpaper and paint them with a thin, dark green paint. When the paint is dry, dip the oars in stain and towel them dry.

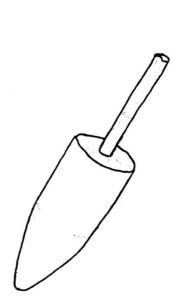

To make the cone-shaped buoys, cut a block 1 $\frac{3}{4}$" long and $\frac{3}{4}$" square. Just round the block, bringing it to a cone on one end. Leave the other end flat and drill a small hole in the center of the flat end, sharpen a short piece of rounded wood and insert it into the hole. Sand the buoy with fine sandpaper to give it a worn look. This type of buoy is usually painted half one color and half another color. You can use any colors you like to paint the buoys. Use the same painting and staining techniques that we used on the sea captain and his crew.

Afterword

I hope that the time and money that you have spent on this book have been well spent. I don't know about you , but with me time and money are always short. What better way to invest them both than in woodcarving? If you are a beginner, just remember that a successful woodcarver doesn't happen overnight. Be patient. As someone once said, "A man can succeed at almost anything for which he has unlimited enthusiasm." If you have any questions or if you want blanks for the projects in this book, contact me at this address:

Mike Shipley
Rt. 1, Box 4490
Dora, MO 65637
(417) 284–3416

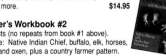 

You are invited to Join the

National Wood Carvers Association
"Some carve their careers: others just chisel"
since 1953

If you have any interest in woodcarving: if you carve wood, create wood sculpture or even just whittle in your spare time, you will enjoy your membership in the National Wood Carvers Association. The non-profit NWCA is the world's largest carving club with over 33,000 members. There are NWCA members in more than 56 countries around the globe.

The Association's goals are to:
- promote wood carving
- foster fellowship among member enthusiasts
- encourage exhibitions and area get togethers
- list sources of equipment and information for the wood carving artist
- provide a forum for carving artists

The NWCA serves as a valuable network of tips, hints and helpful information for the wood carver. Membership is only $11.00 per year.

Members receive the magazine "Chip Chats" six times a year, free with their membership. "Chip Chats" contains articles, news events, demonstrations of technique, patterns and a full color section showcasing examples of fine craftsmanship. Through this magazine you will be kept up to date on shows and workshops to attend, new products, special offers to NWCA members and other members' activities in your area and around the world.

National Wood Carvers Association
7424 Miami Ave.
Cincinnati, OH 45243

Name: _____
Address: _____
_____

Dues $11.00 per year in USA, $14.00 per year foreign (payable in US Funds)

NEW AND RECENT BOOK TITLES...
...from the experts!

Making Classic Chairs:
A Craftsman's Chippendale Reference
Ron Clarkson & Tom Heller

188 pp. softcover
1-56523-081-7   **$24.95**

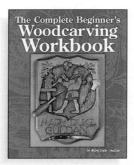

Complete Beginner's Woodcarving Workbook
Mary Duke Guldan

Softcover, 56 pages, 8.5 x 11
1-56523-085-X   **$9.95**

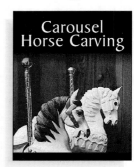

Carousel Horse Carving:
An Instructional Workbook in 1/3 scale
Ken Hughes

Perfect bound, color and black and white,
how-to information, tool lists, full size
pattern included.
1-56523-072-8   **$24.95**

East Weekend Carving Projects
Tina Toney

56 pp. perfect bound, color and black and
white, step-by-step carving and painting
demonstrations patterns.
1-56523-084-1   **$12.95**

Santas and Snowmen:
Carving for Christmas
Tina Toney

56 pp. softcover, Full color.
1-56523-083-3   **$12.95**

**Carving Scrooge and Dickens's
"A Christmas Carol"**
(plus the Olde London Towne scene)
Vince Squeglia

56 pp. 10 complete patterns,
full color gallery included.
1-56523-082-5   **$12.95**

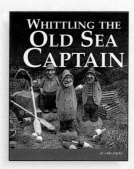

Whittling the Old Sea Captain
Mike Shipley

48 pp. perfect bound, color and black and
white. Includes step-by-step carving &
painting demonstrations, patterns, color
photos of the finished captain crew.
1-56523-075-2   **$12.95**

Free Form Chip Carving
Carol A. Ponte

48 pp. softcover
1-56523-080-9   **$7.95**

Santa Carving With Myron Bowman

56 pp. perfect bound, color and black and
white. Includes step-by-step carving and
painting demonstrations, 11 patterns, color
photos of finished Santas.
1-56523-076-0   **$12.95**

Fox Chapel Publishing Co., Inc.
PO Box 7948
Lancaster, PA 17604-7948

Ordering Information:
Try your favorite book supplier first!
Or see information on following pages to order direct from the publisher.

3 NEW WOODCARVING TITLES FROM DESIREE HAJNY

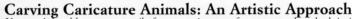

Big Cats: An Artistic Approach

Lions, tigers and jaguars... Oh my! In her second book in a series on carving mammals, renown wildlife carver Desiree Hajny shows you how to take a creative approach to carving the big cats of the savanah, the jungle and the rainforest. Close-up full color photographs of lions, tigers and jaguars in their natural habitat, detailed natural history notes, and anatomy charts provide you with the background information you'll need to *really* understand these beautiful bit cats. You'll even find study sketches from the artist's own notebook! Then focus in on techniques with a chapter devoted specifically to carving, burning and painting big cats. Comparative charts illustrate carving and burning techniques for legs, feet, eyes, ears, noses and mouths. Detailed pen-and-ink illustrations of the cats' fur show how to create the illusion of fur. Finally, follow Desiree as she demonstrates how to carve, burn and paint a miniature version of a lion. More than 90 full color photographs cover the entire process in spectacular detail.

Desiree even includes patterns for six big cat projects. Carve a lioness prowling while draped over a rock outcropping, or a tiger stepping quietly through the jungle. Two patterns featuring cubs—one of a cub with its mother's tail clamped playfully in its mouth and one of a cub being carried by its mother—are also included.

ISBN# 1-56523-071-X
Order Now! $14.95 retail

Carving Caricature Animals: An Artistic Approach

You won't be able to stop a smile from crossing your face as you take a look inside the world of animal caricature with carver Desiree Hajny. Through clearly written text and carefully drawn illustrations, Desiree teaches you how to focus in on the best features to caricature on any animal. Her artistic insight into caricature is balanced out by charts featuring carving techniques and a step-by-step demonstration on how to carve a lop-eared bunny with ears long enough to trip over. Use any one of her full-page charts on carving procedures to isolate the techniques for carving everything from eyes and ears to tails and feet. The step-by-step demonstration includes more than 50 full color photographs to guide you through the basics of caricature carving, burning and painting.

Desiree rounds out her book on caricature carving with eight ready-to-use caricature patterns featuring some of today's most popular animals. You'll find one of the most stubborn-looking mules around, laid-back bobcat, a spotted appaloose horse, a disappearing rabbit, a growling junk yard dog, and an otter doing the back float. She also includes instructions on how to alter these patterns to create endless animal caricatures of your choice.

ISBN# 1-56523-074-4
Order Now! $14.95 retail

Carving Small Animals: An Artistic Approach

In her third book in her series on carving mammals, Desiree Hajny shows you an artistic approach to carving some of our favorite *smaller* mammals—specifically mischievous raccoons, cautious rabbits and acrobatic squirrels. You'll find reference photos showing these animals in their natural habitat, natural history notes, tips on how to conduct your own research and Desiree's own insights into the art of woodcarving. A chapter on technique addresses how to carve, burn and paint small animals. Clearly illustrated charts focus in on hard-to-carve areas, such as eyes, ears, noses and feet. She even shows you the basics of designing realistic small animal carvings through color-coded anatomical charts that show bone movement and weight distribution. A step-by-step demonstration with 85 full color photographs on carving, burning, and painting a standing cottontail—techniques that a carver can use on any small animal carving—completes this outstanding book on carving small animals.

Use the four patterns Desiree includes in her book to carve a raccoon family, a standing cottontail, a balancing gray squirrel or a red squirrel eating a nut. You can also alter these patterns using Desiree's detailed instructions to create new small animal patterns of your own.

ISBN# 1-56523-073-6
Order Now! $14.95 retail

Mammals: An Artistic Approach

"Carvers will learn to carve realistic North American mammals–deer, bear and otters in this informative 150 page book. Techniques for both hand and power carvers are presented. Color painting section. Patterns plus much needed info on texturing and woodburning in the round."

ISBN #1-56523-036-1 $19.95